MW01289693

# Greater Than a Tourist Book
## Series
## Reviews from Readers

I think the series is wonderful and beneficial for tourists to get information before visiting the city.

-Seckin Zumbul, Izmir Turkey

I am a world traveler who has read many trip guides but this one really made a difference for me. I would call it a heartfelt creation of a local guide expert instead of just a guide.

-Susy, Isla Holbox, Mexico

New to the area like me, this is a must have!

-Joe, Bloomington, USA

This is a good series that gets down to it when looking for things to do at your destination without having to read a novel for just a few ideas.

-Rachel, Monterey, USA

Good information to have to plan my trip to this destination.

-Pennie Farrell, Mexico

Great ideas for a port day.

-Mary Martin USA

Aptly titled, you won't just be a tourist after reading this book. You'll be greater than a tourist!

-Alan Warner, Grand Rapids, USA

Even though I only have three days to spend in San Miguel in an upcoming visit, I will use the author's suggestions to guide some of my time there. An easy read - with chapters named to guide me in directions I want to go.

-Robert Catapano, USA

Great insights from a local perspective! Useful information and a very good value!

-Sarah, USA

This series provides an in-depth experience through the eyes of a local. Reading these series will help you to travel the city in with confidence and it'll make your journey a unique one.

-Andrew Teoh, Ipoh, Malaysia

# GREATER THAN A TOURIST- NASHVILLE TENNESSEE USA

*50 Travel Tips from a Local*

Elise Tedeschi

Cover designed by: Ivana Stamenkovic
Cover Image: https://pixabay.com/photos/nashville-tennessee-downtown-2290081/

CZYK Publishing Since 2011.

Greater Than a Tourist

Lock Haven, PA
All rights reserved.

ISBN: 9781698263311

# >TOURIST

## 50 TRAVEL TIPS FROM A LOCAL

# BOOK DESCRIPTION

Are you excited about planning your next trip? Do you want to try something new? Would you like some guidance from a local? If you answered yes to any of these questions, then this Greater Than a Tourist book is for you. Greater Than a Tourist-Nashville, Tennessee, USA by Elise Tedeschi offers the inside scoop on the booming city of Nashville. Most travel books tell you how to travel like a tourist. Although there is nothing wrong with that, as part of the Greater Than a Tourist series, this book will give you travel tips from someone who has lived at your next travel destination.

In these pages, you will discover advice that will help you throughout your stay. This book will not tell you exact addresses or store hours but instead will give you excitement and knowledge from a local that you may not find in other smaller print travel books.

Travel like a local. Slow down, stay in one place, and get to know the people and culture. By the time you finish this book, you will be eager and prepared to travel to your next destination.

Inside this travel guide book you will find:

- Insider tips from a local.

- Packing and planning list.

- List of travel questions to ask yourself or others while traveling.

- A place to write your travel bucket list.

# OUR STORY

Traveling is a passion of the Greater than a Tourist book series creator. Lisa studied abroad in college, and for their honeymoon Lisa and her husband toured Europe. During her travels to Malta, an older man tried to give her some advice based on his own experience living on the island since he was a young boy. She was not sure if she should talk to the stranger but was interested in his advice. When traveling to some places she was wary to talk to locals because she was afraid that they weren't being genuine. Through her travels, Lisa learned how much locals had to share with tourists. Lisa created the Greater Than a Tourist book series to help connect people with locals. A topic that locals are very passionate about sharing.

# TABLE OF CONTENTS

# DEDICATION

This book is dedicated to a dear friend of mine who lives fearlessly and inspires me to reach for the stars no matter the circumstances. Keep shining your light, M.

# ABOUT THE AUTHOR

Elise was born and raised in Nashville, TN. She loves spending time with family and sharing conversations over a cup of coffee. She is always up for an adventure, especially if it consists of nature or new experiences.

# HOW TO USE THIS BOOK

The *Greater Than a Tourist* book series was written by someone who has lived in an area for over three months. The goal of this book is to help travelers either dream or experience different locations by providing opinions from a local. The author has made suggestions based on their own experiences. Please check before traveling to the area in case the suggested places are unavailable.

**Travel Advisories**: As a first step in planning any trip abroad, check the Travel Advisories for your intended destination.
https://travel.state.gov/content/travel/en/traveladvisories/traveladvisories.html

# FROM THE PUBLISHER

Traveling can be one of the most important parts of a person's life. The anticipation and memories that you have are some of the best. As a publisher of the Greater Than a Tourist, as well as the popular *50 Things to Know* book series, we strive to help you learn about new places, spark your imagination, and inspire you. Wherever you are and whatever you do I wish you safe, fun, and inspiring travel.

Lisa Rusczyk Ed. D.
CZYK Publishing

# WELCOME TO
## > TOURIST

*"It is in all of us to defy expectations. To go into the world and to be brave and to want, to need, to hunger for adventures. To embrace change and chance and risk so that we may breathe and know what it is to be free."*

-Mae Chevrette

As a native of Nashville, I believe it is only fair to let you in on some much needed secrets to navigate in city life. From the busyness of Honky Tonk central, to serene locations to gaze on our ever-growing skyline, I hope this can be the friendly guide you turn to. Let's go exploring!

Nashville
Tennessee, USA

# 1. WELCOME TO YOUR HUMBLE NASHVILLIAN ABODE

Finding the perfect place to stay while being in the heart of the city can be a little tricky. If you are like me, you prefer cutting the cost of lodging in order to give yourself some extra spending money. In this case, there are many luxurious, yet, affordable Air BNBs in the bustling heart of Nashville. All you have to do is download the Air BNB app and search 'Nashville, TN'. On the contrary, if you enjoy living like royalty while on vacation, Nashville has a couple perfect accommodating hotels. The Hermitage Hotel, lodging visitors since 1910, is known for its fine architecture and rich history. Another stunningly structured hotel was once known as Nashville's local train station. Union Station, each brick full of more history than the other, is classy, while at the same time encompassing the true essence of southern hospitality. Both hotels start at $365 per night. If you are interested in a more modern, upscale Nashville stay, the Westin, Hutton, or Omni will be your dream come true. They are located in the heart of downtown with magnificent views and very sleek, minimal décor. As a few of the hottest picks for Nashville lodging, their rooms start at $500 per night.

# Nashville
# Climate

| | High | Low |
|---|---|---|
| January | 47 | 29 |
| February | 52 | 32 |
| March | 62 | 40 |
| April | 71 | 48 |
| May | 79 | 57 |
| June | 87 | 65 |
| July | 90 | 70 |
| August | 89 | 68 |
| September | 83 | 62 |
| October | 72 | 49 |
| November | 61 | 40 |
| December | 51 | 32 |

**GreaterThanaTourist.com**

Temperatures are in Fahrenheit degrees.
Source: NOAA

# 2. GAYLORD OPRYLAND RESORT

With a water park, restaurants, boat rides, and more, the Gaylord Opryland Resort is a one stop shop. It offers three different kinds of rooms – the guest room, the parlor, and the deluxe. They are differing in price depending on the room view and package you choose. You can either solely book a room or you can choose a package that includes passes to Soundwaves, the brand new waterpark taking over four acres of the hotel grounds. It is exclusive to hotel guests and parties. If you are not rooming at the resort, outside guests are permitted to walk around and enjoy the restaurants and shops. Opryland has nine acres of indoor gardens and a pond that flows through the lobby. The hotel offers boat rides along the pond, creating a calm, scenic adventure for the whole family.

# 3. MOVE YOUR CAR, LOSE YOUR SPOT

Parking in downtown Nashville is a beast of its own. With more and more tourists visiting every day, the streets remain clogged. It is very rare to find a parking spot among the side street spaces, so if you are ever-so-lucky, count it a small victory! When it comes to on-street parking, make sure you find the parking meter associated with the parking spot and read all the signs around it to keep from getting your car towed away. Nashville meters range at about $0.50 for the first twenty minutes. Depending on what the nearby signs read, most meters require payment anywhere between thirty minutes to two hours of being parked. Something exciting to keep in mind is that the meters only charge between 8:00am-6:00pm, Monday through Saturday, any other time and you have successfully found free, on-street parking! If you don't have much luck finding on-street parking, there are quite a few government/public parking garages and lots. Unfortunately, pricing fluctuates so often on these locations depending on events that are taking place downtown at the time or the time of day. Now, I'm going to let you in on a secret. Sometimes, I just pay the price of a parking garage for the sake of my own sanity. It can be worth avoiding the stress of walking miles or having to parallel park in the middle of traffic.

# 4. NASHVILLE TRAFFIC

I think it is safe to say nobody really likes sitting in traffic. Long, exhausting hours of getting absolutely nowhere. Nashville highways and interstates are becoming notorious for traffic jams. Almost everywhere you turn is labeled with a sign stating, "under construction," or "road work ahead." Interstate 440, which is the main highway to connect you to downtown, has been under construction for about a year now. They are in the process of expanding, which will ultimately help the issue of feeling overcrowded. But for now, plan ahead and make sure you know where you are going, otherwise you will be in a jam longer than anticipated. Bring games to play in the car and good tunes to make the trip more enjoyable!

## 5. "THESE BOOTS WERE MADE FOR WALKIN'"

Do not let the fact that you are in a city intimidate you. While Nashville is growing, it is not as big as your average city. To get from one side of downtown to the other is only about a fifteen minute walk. If you are capable and willing, walking is one of the best modes of transportation in Nashville, so make sure to bring your walking shoes. Just think, you can sightsee while on your way to your next destination. That's killing two birds with one stone!

# 6. DOWNTOWN TRANSPORTATION

The most popular way to get around downtown Nashville is using either Uber or Lyft. There are drivers everywhere, ready at all times, to pick up you and your group and get you where you need to be. They will charge more on weekends or after events considering the larger flow of people. Keep in mind that you will have to tip your driver. Another way to get around is by bus. There are two bus lines that make their way around Nashville. One is called Music City Central, also known as Nashville MTA. It is located on Charlotte Avenue providing ninety-six routes. MTA charges $2 for a quick ride, or for $4 you can have access to an all-day pass. The second bus line is the Music City Circuit. The best part about this one is that it is completely free! It has only two routes, but they ride through some of the most popular areas.

# 7. BIKES AND SCOOTERS

If you are more inclined to physical activity, you can find many 'Rent-A-Bike' stations throughout the streets of downtown. This is the perfect way to enjoy a leisurely ride through the city at your own pace. For a more stop and go experience, Bird and Lyft provide scooters. If you see one laying on the sidewalk, it is yours to take. All you have to do is download the appropriate mobile app for payment and activation. Be careful of traffic, though! Scooters have been known to be the more dangerous route when rolling around downtown. Scoot at your own risk! It isn't all that dangerous just as long as you are alert and aware of your surroundings. Bikes and scooters are just different ways to enjoy getting around the city without having to sit in traffic. They are also perfect ways to enjoy the weather as you are riding through the hustle and bustle of downtown.

# 8. EXCHANGING CURRENCY

The Nashville International Airport (BNA) does provide currency exchange options through SunTrust Bank and Wright Travel, both located on ticketing level. If you are looking to exchange your currency outside of the airport, Wells Fargo, Avenue Bank, First Tennessee Bank, and Bank of America provide these services. They are all located in downtown Nashville. Some ATMs do charge a currency exchange fee. For more details, visit the bank websites.

# 9. MUSIC CITY TOURS

Nashville has many musical history sites to explore. The Grand Ole Opry and The Ryman are Nashville's top performing stages. Each have rich history behind them and provide an array of culture in the country music field. For even more insight on country music, the Country Music Hall of Fame is the place to go. It consists of many exhibits and members such as Garth Brooks, Dolly Parton, Johnny Cash, and more. Speaking of Johnny Cash, if you are a fan of his, Nashville is home to the Johnny Cash museum. This museum holds the largest collection of artifacts that belonged to him. On a more instrumental note, visit Gibson and experience how Gibson guitars are made. For a more classical tour, take a step into the beautiful architecture and acoustics of Nashville's Schermerhorn Symphony Hall.

# 10. HISTORICAL TOURS

From president Andrew Jackson's home to the Greek Parthenon, Nashville has a wide range of historical sites and landmarks. Yes, you heard correctly. There is an exact replica of the Greek Parthenon right in the center of downtown Nashville. Throughout the tour, you will encounter a forty-one-foot-tall, golden Athena. Journeying on, the south is known for their grand plantations, two of which are located in the heart of Nashville. The Belle Meade Plantation and the Cheekwood Estate and Gardens uncover the beauty and history of life in the Civil War era. To see artifacts and memorabilia of the Civil War, visit the newly constructed Tennessee State Museum. You can even tour Civil War fortification, Fort Negley, where the Union forces were occupied. All right here in Nashville, Tennessee. The view of Nashville from Fort Negley is one you will not want to miss. Nashville is pridefully the home to the Tennessee state capitol, where they hold tours Monday through Friday. This will give you an inside scoop on what it is like to be a part of the Tennessee General Assembly and seeing exactly where the governor's office is. Isn't it cool that you can tour such a historical building while being only a few blocks away from the busyness of the city life?

# 11. TOURS ON WHEELS

While walking tours are fun and insightful, you may prefer a tour that drives you around everywhere. If that is the case, you're in luck! Nashville offers quite a few tours on wheels. In a more historical light, Old Town Trolley Tours will take you around downtown, stopping at different museums and allowing you to get on or off whenever you please. If you see a big pink bus, hop on the NashTrash Tour for a fun filled, comedic take on the history of Nashville.

# 12. THE TENNESSEE STATE MUSEUM

With a brand new facility, just opening in October of 2018, the Tennessee State Museum has many permanent exhibits that offer a lot of history. These exhibits consist of Natural History, First Peoples, Forging A Nation, The Civil War and Reconstruction, and Tennessee Transforms. Providing so much to see and learn in the permanent exhibits, there are also temporary exhibits that are very insightful. Make sure you check the website to see what will be on display while you are visiting. There is a hands on Children's Gallery for ages 3-8, giving them a chance to learn and explore in a way that best suits them. Tennessee has a lot to offer when it comes to history and the Tennessee State Museum is the perfect place to learn all about it.

# 12. NASHVILLE WEATHER

The climate in Nashville is very pleasant between April and October with much warmer temperatures in the summer months. This is when the streets are full of musical acts and people having a good time. There is not really a time of year when it rains more or less, so be ahead of the game and bring an umbrella or rain jacket just in case. We rarely see snow throughout the winter and temperatures will dip down to 20°F in the earlier months of the year. When it does snow here, most of Nashville shuts down as we are not fully equipped with snow clearing machinery, so plan accordingly. Like anywhere else, the weather in Nashville has a mind of its own.

# 13. OUTDOOR FUN

Looking to get out of the city for a day? Just outside of Nashville are a few beautiful parks and greenways. Some of which contain serene lakes and others are occupied by boats and jet skis. Radnor Lake is known for its superb hiking trails around the lake. A few of its trails take you to great heights with amazing views while Percy Priest lake is where people go to spend a day on the water. Percy Priest lake has marinas that offer boat storage and amenities. If you do not have a boat, they do offer boat rental services by hour or by day! This includes jet skis, pontoon party boats, fishing boats, and ski boats. You can also rent the proper safety gear as well as inner tubes, water skis, and wakeboards. There is a "beach" area where the tide runs up to the sand. On the contrary, there is a rocky area along the lake with picnic tables, where my family loves to spend summer holidays grilling and then cooling off by going for a spin on the jet skis! If you are up for an adventure, take a boat around the lake and try to find the perfect diving cliffs and enjoy showing off some cool flips to your family and friends! Percy Priest also has campgrounds ranging from $14-$24 depending on the location, as well as a $3 fee per person per day. You can also bring your fishing gear and set up on any of the banks to catch anything from bass, to catfish or trout! Then, you can clean up your catch and grill it while overlooking the beauty of the lake. Percy Warner Park is another land park that has beautiful stone steps that are rewarding to climb and rest at the top with a quaint view. Percy Warner offers hiking trails, mountain bike trails, horse trails, dog parks, overlooks, and picnic areas. This is the perfect place to spend a sunny, fall day. For a greenway experience, Shelby Bottoms park, located in East Nashville, is populated with bikers, running squads, baseball fields, greenways and a view of the Cumberland River, where a fun time is had by all. Bring a baseball and a bat or a kickball and rally people hanging around the park for a fun game! Lastly, as Nashville's only completely public waterpark, Nashville Shores is 385 acres of family fun. It includes waterslides, treetop adventures, lakeside lodging, and much more. On a hot summer day, nothing is more refreshing than water slides and wave pools!

# 14. THE NASHVILLE ZOO AT GRASSMERE

Let's go on a safari! The Nashville Zoo houses 365 different animal species. While you can only look at many of them from a distance, there are a few special animals that get to be a part of the petting zoo. Other than animals, the Nashville Zoo offers many more attractions for kids, such as a vastly structured jungle gym, merry go round, zipline, and the historic Grassmere home. The zoo is accommodating to all different ages and groups. Though it is closed during the winter, it is guaranteed to be a fun time had by all in the spring and summer months.

# 15. FREE EVENTS

Traveling on a low budget can sound impossible but it can be very doable while still being enjoyable. Nashville natives thrive off of free events in the area and you can, too, if you do your research ahead of time and check out what's going when you will be visiting. Here are a few to start. In the fall, from August to September, is a free music festival known as Live On The Green (LOTG). It is held at Public

Square Park and features, local, regional, and national artists. Right down the street is the Nashville Farmer's Market. You can pick up fresh produce, flowers, and handmade trinkets. When you're done shopping, step into the food court for a variety of restaurants. Going in to the evening with your fresh produce from the market, you can make your way to Arrington Vineyards for a relaxing picnic. Set your blanket at the top of the hill, overlooking the vineyard and sip on their exclusive AV wine while the sun settles down for the night.

# 16. LIVE MUSIC

One of the many perks of visiting Music City is that there is live music on just about every street corner. You will not have to look hard or long for musical entertainment. Being downtown, you can hear music coming from hundreds of different directions. Walking down Lower Broadway or Honky Tonk Highway, restaurants and bars are booming with karaoke or local bands putting on shows for visitors that can easily be heard from the streets. A few popular restaurants on Lower Broadway that provide free, live music are Margaritaville, Acme Feed and Seed, and Hard Rock Café. Not far from Broadway, located in The Gulch is a dine and dance club called Sambuca. It is a far cry from honky tonk as it provides you with a dim lighting, classic/southern rock dining experience. Sambuca is a great place to stop for a drink or laidback dinner. Just down the road from Sambuca is Rudy's Jazz Room. Rudy's is a late-night speakeasy with outstanding local jazz performers and New Orleans cuisine. I love spending my evenings at Rudy's after a long day of work, or for you, a long day of touring! It creates the perfect atmosphere to sit back and relax while sipping on a cocktail and being entertained by superbly smooth, live jazz arrangements. My friends and I like to dress up and pretend we're going back in time for the evening when we go to Rudy's. It creates the opportunity to get even more lost in the dreaminess of it all, that is, if you are in to jazz!

# 17. UPSCALE SHOPPING

Nashville offers a wonderful range of upscale shopping locations. If you like to treat yourself on vacation, take a stroll around The Gulch for upscale boutiques and shops, such as Urban Outfitters, Two Old Hippies, e.Allen Boutique, and Lucchese Bootmaker. 21st Avenue South also has very trendy, locally owned shops like Posh Boutique, The Impeccable Pig, and Native + Nomad.  Why not spend a day finding one of a kind pieces found only in Nashville? 21st Avenue also has some hip dining options. Pizza Perfect, San Antonio Taco Co (known as SATCO to us natives), and Taco Mama are a few popular locations. Just outside of Nashville is The Mall At Green Hills where you can find stores like Madewell, Louis Vuitton, and Burberry. In the opposite direction, the Opry Mills Mall houses Coach, Michael Kors, Swarovski, and much more.

# 18. BOOTS, BOOTS, AND MORE BOOTS!

Are you a Nashville tourist but feel like you don't quite fit in the downtown, honky tonk scene yet? Do you feel like cowboy boots just might do the trick…but you don't own a pair? Well make sure you stop by Boot Country, Boot Factory Outlet, or Nashville Cowboy and you will go from having no cowboy boots to having three pairs for the price of one! That's right, you heard me correctly. Those three locations have an ongoing sale "Buy 1 Pair, Get 2 Pairs FREE!" Wander around the shop and find the pair that makes you feel the most at home in Nashville. Now you, your family, and your friends will all fit right in to honky tonk central, looking ready to take on the country music stage.

# 19. DRESSING AS A TOURIST

Most of the time, tourists in Nashville stick out like sore thumbs. They are usually seen wearing genuine leather cowboy boots and a big ole' cowboy hat. While Nashville is known for country music, it is rare that you will see a native decked out in country, farming attire. If you are comfortable with Nashville natives knowing you aren't from around here, don't be afraid to rock your "southern attire." On the contrary, if you want to blend in with everyday Nashvillians, try wearing casual clothes and you may succeed in go unnoticed as a tourist.

# 20. NASHVILLE BRUNCH

Walking around all morning and ready for an early afternoon pick me up? Marché Artisan Foods and Stay Golden are two very cozy and welcoming brunch spots offering delicious menus. Marché is a European-style café located in East Nashville while Stay Golden is a roastery in Berry Hill. For a more exotic experience, Sinema is an old theater house turned restaurant that offers superb brunch specials on Saturdays and Sundays, known as Bottomless Brunch. Though Nashville has many very delicious brunch locations, those are few Nashville native favorites.

# 21. LOCAL COFFEE SHOPS

If you are not looking to eat and just want a nice cup of coffee to get you on your way, local roasters are popping up everywhere in the heart of Nashville. To name a few, CREMA, Steadfast Coffee, Red Bicycle, and Barista Parlor are fan favorites. CREMA provides a cozy, rustic vibe while Steadfast is millennial minded and to the point. Red Bicycle serves delicious crepes along with their high-end roasted coffee in a friendly atmosphere. Finally, Barista Parlor in East Nashville is very hip and spacious, providing natural light and fresh air as their garage doors are always open. Keep in mind that coffee shops are almost as popular as live music in Nashville, so you won't have to look far to find the perfect place to enjoy a cup of joe.

# 22. TIME TO EAT

As a tourist, it is important to eat at locally owned restaurants that you won't find anywhere else. Nashville has a plethora of exclusive places in that category. For a big juicy burger paired with a vast beer selection, The Pharmacy Burger Parlor and Beer Garden should be at the top of your list. On a different note, for entertainment while dining, House of Cards brings a magical approach to your evening. With a strict dress code and $$$$ menu, sit back and enjoy a top of the line magic show. Providing a more laid back entertaining dining atmosphere, Mangia Nashville is like walking in to a big, Italian family dinner. Each weekend, they transform in to feast nights where you will indulge in a six course meal. With The Godfather playing on the screen, dancing is sure to happen. You can even step outside for a game of bocce ball on their outdoor court. Rather have barbecue? Be sure to try Martin's Bar-B-Que Joint; pulled pork at its finest! Sometimes they even open the pig pit and allow customers to watch the process of pulling the pork. Now, a trip to Nashville is not complete without a visit to the infamous Loveless Café. It is not in the heart of Nashville, but it is a must. Most popular for their southern breakfast menu and homemade biscuits and jam, Loveless Café has served countless country music artists. Who knows? You may even see an artist while YOU visit the restaurant. The wait can be long so make sure to arrive early.

# 23. TALK TO YOUR SERVERS

The exciting thing about visiting Music City is that most people you meet here are musical artists. A lot of the time, they are disguised as waiters or waitresses. When sitting down at a restaurant with your family or friends, start talking to your server and see why they're working there and what brought them to Nashville. Majority of the time it will be music that inspired them to make the move here. Do not be afraid to ask for their artist name! I am sure they would love to share their music with you. If you're feeling in the giving mood, leave them a nice tip to help them get along in their career! Wouldn't it be cool if they get famous, you can say you knew them in their early years? I love discovering new music and new musical artists. I have met so many artists while eating at restaurants and trust me, they love when you ask about them! So, you get to enjoy a nice meal while learning about new music. Talk to your servers and you will not be disappointed!

## 24. NASHVILLE HOT CHICKEN

Hot chicken, made famous by Nashville, is a tourist must. Even if you don't like hot chicken, you have to try it just to say you've had "Nashville Hot Chicken." Hattie B's, Party Fowl, and Prince's Hot Chicken offer some of the best in town. You don't have to get the hottest option, but for the adventurous type and for the full experience, it is recommended. Keep in mind that even if it says "mild," it will still have a little spice to it. The Nashville Hot Chicken experience is one you will not forget!

# 25. BARS, BAR CRAWLS, AND PEDAL TAVERNS, OH MY!

Downtown Nashville has too many bars to count. Many of which are owned by country music artists. Luke Bryan's 32 Bridge, Jason Aldean's Kitchen and Rooftop Bar, FGL House by Florida Georgia Line, AJ's Good Time Bar by Alan Jackson, John Rich's Redneck Riviera, Dierks Bentley's Whiskey Row, and Kid Rock's Honky Tonk Steakhouse are just to name a few. The Big Bang Dueling Piano Bar creates a unique experience while sipping on a strong drink, forgetting about the outside world. Skull's Rainbow Room, Legends Corner, The Stage, and Bourbon Street Blues and Boogie Bar are the bars that you have to visit solely to have good time. Music City provides multiple bar and pub crawls if you're interested. They are always changing so the best thing to do is research before you come. Pedal Taverns are a tourist favorite. What sounds more exciting than fifteen people pedaling down Broadway while drinking and screaming? Not much. The Pedal Taverns are BYOB. They provide the cooler, cups, and ice and you provide the alcohol.

# 26. ROOFTOP BARS

If you want to enjoy an exciting view of the city while sipping a glass of wine or shooting Fireball whiskey, check out one of Nashville's many rooftop bars. Climb up to the top floor of Acme Feed and Seed for a view of Broadway and the Cumberland River. L27 at the Westin Hotel comes fully equipped with a pool lounge and gorgeous view of the skyline. L.A. Jackson is a popular rooftop hangout location in The Gulch. It has a welcoming atmosphere serving southern dishes, craft beer, cocktails, and wine. More than not, restaurants in downtown Nashville have rooftop access. Don't be afraid to ask your server about it!

# 27. HAPPY HOUR

Happy hour ranges from 3:00 to 7:00. Restaurants in East Nashville, Eighth Avenue, Berry Hill, and many more locations, succumb to the half price drink trend. You can order a tasty appetizer before dinner while enjoying a drink you don't have to feel guilty for. Some restaurants even offer half price appetizers, so it's a win-win!

# 28. YAZOO BREWING COMPANY

Yazoo Brewing is a Nashville native. Independently owned and operated by Linus and Lisa Hall, its doors opened in 2003 and is doing better than ever today. Providing 10 flagship beers and 5 seasonal brews, they are widely known in the Nashville area. They offer evening tours on Wednesday-Saturday. It is a one of a kind experience allowing you to sample their beers throughout the tour and they gift you with a 5oz souvenir glass to take home.

# 29. OLE SMOKY DISTILLERY AND YEE-HAW BREWING COMPANY

Located on 6th Avenue, Ole Smoky and Yee-Haw have joined forces for what they call "6th and Peabody." 6th and Peabody is guaranteed to be a good time as the location consists of the brewery, distillery, tasting areas, bars, and live entertainment. In visiting the brewery, you will be able to enjoy food from White Duck Taco and Prince's Hot Chicken while sipping on Ole Smoky Moonshine or a Yee-Haw Brewing Co. beer. You are permitted to purchase moonshine and beer to take home with you!

# 30. HONKY TONK AND PRINTER'S ALLEY

Popular for its ambiance, Printer's Alley is just blocks away from the Cumberland River. It is booming with nightclubs and nightlife, where everyone is ready to party. Honky Tonk is where you can find Nudie's Honky Tonk, Honky Tonk Central, and Honky Tonk Brewing Co. You will also find Coyote Ugly Saloon, made popular by tourists. Coyote Ugly Saloon is a more R rated version of Hooters. Tourists love it, so if you are in to that, it is a highly recommended bar. Stay out late and walk around honky tonk and Printer's Alley for more nightlife, more fun times, and memory making guaranteed.

# 31. BACHELORETTE PARTIES

Behind Las Vegas, Nashville is the second most popular destination for bachelorette parties. With the bars, food, and live music, it is easy to see why it is the perfect place for the "last fling before the ring." The Honky Tonk Party Express and Pedal Taverns are the top modes of transportation for bachelorette parties in Nashville. The pedal taverns book up very quickly so make sure you call ahead a few weeks ahead to secure your spot. There are a couple cute nail salons downtown such as Poppy and Monroe, which is a non toxic nail salon, and Polish Nails & Concierge, which is a luxury mobile nail boutique. They can come to you and pamper you and girls right in their mobile. Or there are places like Studio Goddess where you can learn pole dancing, aerial acrobatics, southern swagger, and much more. It is easy for natives to spot bachelorette parties as all members of the party are typically matching in attire and screaming up and down Broadway. Nashville is happy to be part of the last days of your single life and wishes you the very best in your marriage.

# 32. NIGHTLIFE

On the weekends, Nashville comes alive and fills with people, especially at night. It is the perfect opportunity to meet new people and find new places to explore. Bars are booming and everyone is in a happy-go-lucky mood. Be sure to jump on a karaoke stage if you want memories for the books and a night you will not soon forget. If you are not in to the crazy city nightlife scene, stay away from Broadway and Printer's Alley. There are plenty of places just outside the city that are more laid back and less crowded.

# 33. MUSIC ROW

Music Row is a strip located near The Gulch. It is home to many record label companies, recording studios, and radio stations. There are daytime and evening walking tours that equip you with the history and excitement of recording music. RCA Studio B is Nashville's most rich recording studio having worked with artists like Dolly Parton, Elvis Presley, and Willie Nelson.

# 34. SPORTS IN NASHVILLE

From soccer to hockey, Nashville does it all. The Nashville Soccer Club debuted in 2018. You can purchase single game tickets and enjoy a night of MLS. If you prefer football, the NFL team, Tennessee Titans' field is located in Nashville. Catch a home game while you're here and you won't regret it. The Nashville Sounds games, our minor league baseball team, are a fun way to spend a cool summer evening with your friends or family. I enjoy getting a hot dog, funnel cakes, and a scoop of ice cream, which happens to come in a little plastic baseball helmet, to make the most of the experience. Or you could always just get peanuts and cracker jacks! And last but not least, when it comes to hockey in Nashville, you do not even have to like hockey for it to be a fun time. We are a proud home to our Nashville

Predators. Leftover tickets are usually available the day of the games and these are games you won't want to miss. It is a fun time had by all as the streets of Nashville fill up and are overtaken by a sea of gold and navy blue. These are my favorite games to go as the arena is packed with happy, exciting energy and people ready to cheer on our players. Let's go Preds!

# 35. IN THE SOUTH, EVERYONE IS NICE

Nashville will welcome you with a big, warm greeting. Everyone will say hi or maybe even overstep and give you a hug. Southerners are almost always in the mood for a "get-to-know-you" conversation, so sit back and stay awhile! Do not be intimidated by the smiles and nice gestures, it is our way of saying "Welcome to the south!"

# 36. SOUTHERN SLANG

"Bless your heart." These are typically words you don't want to hear from people in the south. It usually means you've done something completely wrong or you lack common sense but it's the southern way of letting you know nicely. If you are thirsty for a nice glass of sweet tea, make sure you specify that you want sweet tea. Otherwise, if you ask for iced tea, that's what you'll get and there will be nothing sweet about it.

# 37. NATIVES ARE RARE

These days, it is rare that you will encounter an authentic Nashville native. Nashville is becoming more and more populated by outsiders. It will be a shining moment if you meet someone who was born and raised right here in Nashville, Tennessee. Make this a game on your trip and try to find at least one native as you meet new people!

# 38. FOR THE KIDS

If you are bringing kids with you on your trip, Nashville has so many fun places for them to experience. The Adventure Science Center is hard to miss, as it has a large pyramid structured on the roof of it's building. Here, kids have the opportunity to learn through hands-on experiments and exhibits. It can even be enjoyed by adults, making it the perfect place to go for the family. For outdoor fun, visit Fannie Mae Dees Park, also known as the dragon park for its large dragon structure for kids to play on. The Bicentennial Mall, located near the farmer's market, has fountains that stay on during the warmer months, creating a fun-filled water experience for children.

# 39. NASHVILLE THEATERS

Touring Broadway shows make their way to the Tennessee Performing Arts Center (TPAC) stage, located in the heart of downtown Nashville. Local talent, such as Circle Players, also perform on the stages of TPAC. For a more kid-friendly atmosphere, the Nashville Children's Theater offers a light atmosphere and family-friendly productions. You can catch more shows at The Dark Horse Theater, Belcourt Theater, Street Theater Company, and Shamblin Theater. Chaffin's Barn and Miss Marple's Dinner Theater will provide you with dining and theater entertainment. If you enjoy theater and are interested in seeing a show during your visit, Nashville holds many different options.

# 40. BEST TIMES TO VISIT NASHVILLE

Spring to Fall is the best time to visit Nashville. Everyone is outside, windows and doors are open. Broadway becomes a concert venue and all of the bars up and down the road are the hottest hangout spots. The night life becomes the morning life and there is no in between. The weather is comfortable and perfect for the free events and live music that the seasons hold. Winter is a gorgeous time to come as well, the only downfall is that most shops, stores, and restaurants close their doors if encountered with a flurry. Nashville runs on outdoor events, so if you are not wanting all of your time visiting the city spent at either restaurants or shops, the colder months may not be the most ideal time to come. Nashville really is enjoyable all year round, there is just more that will keep you busy during the warmer months!

# 41. CMA FEST

If you make your way to Nashville in the summer, you may encounter the largest music festival held here. The CMA fest is when many well-known country music artists perform on the big stage and the streets of Nashville are jam packed with fans. There are after parties and charity events that also take place as a part of the festival. If you don't buy tickets to the festival, you can still get downtown, it will just be very busy and hard to navigate. If you are into country music, plan your trip ahead of time and purchase tickets to experience this fun filled weekend.

# 42. EVENTS IN THE PARK

If being outdoors is a hobby of yours, Nashville's parks have countless free events on their grounds. Shakespeare In The Park puts a fun twist on Shakespearean stories from August to September. Bring a picnic meal and enjoy the show! Every Saturday evening in Centennial Park, June to August, you can experience Big Band Dancing In The Park. It is an evening full of swing dancing, a live big band, and dance lessons. Join in with hundreds of others dancing the night away and let it transport you in to the world of swing, tango, waltz and many more styles of dance. The best part is that it is completely free! Centennial Park almost always has a free event happening. Sometimes, there are food truck festivals, African street festivals, craft fairs, etc., so stop by and see what you can find. Even if there isn't an event, Centennial Park is a gorgeous place to walk around. Venture through the garden and around the pond. You may even see a few ducks swimming around in the pond! Bring a book or a frisbee and enjoy a gorgeous day in the fields of Centennial Park.

# 43. PAINTED WALLS

Believe it or not, Nashville is well known for its painted murals. So much so, that Nashville has created a mural tour for visitors to embark on. Nashville Mural Tours stops at all of the painted walls and gives you the opportunity to see the artwork and take pictures. They have an option for Single Reservations consisting of a two and a half hour tour for $35 or they have a two and a half hour Private Tour for $350. Private Tours are typically booked for birthday parties or bachelorette parties. It just goes to show how many murals there are considering the tour will be two and a half hours. Believe it or not, there are lines of people waiting to take pictures at most of these murals, which could prolong the tour, so plan accordingly. Nashville Mural Tours also offers photography services, making sure you get the perfect snapshots with your family and friends! There is an option for professional photography and editing, providing you with 50+ portraits, or there is a smartphone photo option. There will be a worker available to take pictures for you using either their smartphone or yours, providing as many pictures as you would like. The artists that have painted these murals are extremely talented and have, without a doubt, left their mark. So, hop on the tour bus for a couple hours of exploring the city's artwork. I have lived in this city since birth and it has been very exciting to watch as the city fills with more and more murals displaying how people express themselves through art. I have never done this tour, but driving around downtown, you can easily spot murals just about anywhere. Jump out of your car or uber really quickly and pose for a picture in front of the masterpiece you find! Or, you can find a list of murals, along with their locations, on google and take your family and friends on your own tour. That way, you can enjoy the paintings and artwork at your own pace while at the same time, feeling less guilty for paying a price to do so. This is something that even Nashville natives enjoy doing. I would almost consider this a "must do" because the artwork is so stunning and vibrant, it would be a shame to miss out on seeing them for yourself.

# 44. EXTRA FUN

For more active fun and a break from walking the busy streets of the city, head over to Pinewood Social for a delicious meal and an upscale game of bowling. Pinewood has a very cool, hip environment. The dining area is very open welcoming. This is the place to go for cozy, laid back fun. Recently added to Nashville's entertainment is Topgolf. Practice your swings for points while filling up on yummy food from the sports bar. At Topgolf, you do not have to be a professional golfer in order to enjoy your time there.

The only golfing I have ever done is miniature golf but when I go to Topgolf, I feel empowered as I swing the club and watch the ball fly miles away. Who knows? Maybe you could be the next Tiger Woods! The wait for a bay can be long so plan accordingly. Just around the corner from Topgolf is Music City Indoor Go Karts. With their karts reaching 40 mph, it makes for a fun filled, competitive time with friends and family. They also offer a fun, indoor miniature golf course where you can kill time while waiting for your turn on the race track. For more leisurely fun around Nashville, catch a horse drawn carriage and let it take you for a stroll through the city. This is a relaxing way to enjoy the fresh air while still being a part of the downtown Nashville scene.

## 45. SATISFY YOUR SWEET TOOTH

Nashville has many options when it comes to sweets. If you have spent a long, hot day touring the city, stop in Mike's Ice Cream on 2nd Avenue for homemade ice cream. I love their milkshakes. They are not too sweet but still hit the spot! You can also try Jeni's Splendid Ice Cream, located in 12th South and East Nashville, for more exotic ice cream flavors. Jeni's Brown Butter Almond Brittle ice cream is one of their flavors I could eat by the pint. The flavors may sound crazy, but don't let them scare you off. They are destined for greatness! If ice cream is not your fancy, make your way to Savannah's Candy Kitchen for homemade fudge and candies of all sorts. Down the road from Savannah's is Rocket Fizz filled with nostalgic candy and soda pop from days gone by. This is a place with an exciting atmosphere as you are reminded of childhood. It will give you an opportunity to share with your kids what you enjoyed when you were their age. Rocket Fizz has vintage posters and signs hanging up all over the walls that are fun to look at and are also available to purchase! For a giant sugar overload, Five Daughter's Bakery on 12th South is the place to go. They have delicious, mile high donuts, just perfect to fulfill your sweet tooth or act as a meal replacement. They even have seasonal donuts! Five Daughter's is a locally owned bakery, so make sure you stop by!

# 46. FRIST ART MUSEUM

The Frist is Nashville's only visual arts museum. The exhibits are ever changing and rich in culture. Exhibits can be anything from Italian automobiles to Norman Rockwell and Andy Warhol paintings. Or even my personal favorite, "Italian Style: Fashion Since 1945," displaying dresses, suits, shoes, bags, skirts, and more directly from the vintage eras. Ages 18 and younger receive free admission. On the upper level of the museum is a hands-on gallery, known as the Martin ArtQuest Gallery. It is the perfect place for kids and adults to let their creative juices flow.

## 47. HATCH SHOW PRINT

Hatch Show Print is a letterpress that has been in business since 1879. The tour of the press will enlighten you in the poster making process and history of poster culture in Nashville. Hatch Show Print also has an opportunity to do letter press activities with the family. You can purchase posters and even send in a request for custom posters.

## 48. GET TO KNOW JACK

Not far from Nashville is the Jack Daniel's Distillery. Take a walk though Jack Daniel's life and discover how the finest Tennessee whiskey is made. The tour will take you through each step of the process, from starting as water to bottling the whiskey. Have a few sips here and there to determine which is your favorite. After the tour, make your way to the town square for a bite to eat and the Jack Daniel's general store.

# 49. GENERAL JACKSON SHOWBOAT

Being one of the largest showboats ever built, the General Jackson will take you for a ride down the Cumberland River where you will experience dinner and musical performances. From Christmas shows to "Taste Of Tennessee," the shows have a wide range of styles and talent. This includes bluegrass, soul, gospel, and lots of country music. It is recommended that you call ahead of time to make reservations. Come paddle away on the Cumberland river!

# 50. HOMES OF THE STARS GUIDED TOUR

Spend a few hours of your time in Nashville visiting the homes of many Nashville stars. Taylor Swift, Dolly Parton, Reese Witherspoon, Martina McBride, Garth Brooks, and many more, have magnificent homes located in or just outside of Nashville. You are not permitted to enter the homes, but getting an outside view in their beautiful, upscale neighborhoods is hard to beat. Take it all in and pretend you are going to visit them at their home for a nice afternoon tea.

# BONUS 51. NASHVILLE'S FAMOUS CLUSTER

The Goo Goo Cluster, named after the Grand Ole Opry, has become popular in Nashville stores. The factory has been in business since 1912 and produces 20,000 clusters an hour. That's a lot! If you visit the factory, you will have the opportunity to make your very own Goo Goo Cluster and learn a secret recipe from the Dessert Bar. Enjoy one while you are here but make sure you get a box to take home to share with your family and friends.

# BONUS 52. CONCERT VENUES

A lot of the time, street vendors will stand outside concert venues selling leftover tickets. Sometimes it is worth it to indulge. Many artists tour to Nashville's Bridgestone Arena, where the seats are always packed. If you have the opportunity to buy a leftover ticket for a show at the arena, you won't want to miss the offer for you are assured to have a fun evening. As soon as you walk into the arena, the energy of the people around you is so exhilarating! With everybody ready to enjoy an evening of music, sit back and relax or get up and get your feet to dancing! During the warmer months, Ascend Amphitheater is a booming concert venue. With limited assigned seating, the best way to go is general admission lawn seating, providing you with room to dance to the groove of the music. Sometimes the musicians will even wander around the audience, making you close enough to smell their sweat! If you are lucky enough to have a hotel near the amphitheater, you can enjoy the music from your balcony. The Ryman Auditorium is a classic venue and to see a show performed there is close to being considered an honor. The musicians that perform at the Ryman are often humbled and share their gratitude with the audience, creating a sweet, sweet moment. Balcony seating is usually the best way to go at this venue. Floor seating can be risky if you are directly below the balcony, making it a little more difficult to see the stage. Just think of it this way, whether you can see the stage or not, you can hear the music just the same. EXIT/IN is a venue consisting of a standing room only, with minimal balcony space creating a close and intimate atmosphere with other concert goers. This is the place for you if you are in to rock music or up and coming artists. I have been to multiple concerts at each of these venues and it is safe to say that no matter which one you choose, if you enjoy the music, you will definitely have a good time. After all, Nashville is known for its love of music.

# BONUS 53. NASHVILLE SKYLINE

The perfect way to end one of your days in Nashville is to reach a good vantage point to view the skyline. Love Circle provides the perfect ambience to watch the sun set behind the skyline. Bring a blanket and get comfy at the top of the hill. The pedestrian bridge, located in the heart of downtown, is another perfect place to get an up-close view of our beautiful Nashville skyline. Finally, UP, the rooftop lounge, has a stunning view of downtown Nashville. So, enjoy sipping on a drink with friends and family as you relax above the busyness of the streets.

# TOP REASONS TO BOOK THIS TRIP

**Lively Music City Streets:** The streets are always alive and surrounded with music. Every corner is a musical moment waiting to happen.

**Rich History:** Almost everywhere in Nashville has a historical background. Make sure you ask a local if they know anything about the location. Take time to tour the historical sights, it will be worth your while.

**Food:** Nashville provides some of the best fine dining experiences. There are a lot of local, one of a kind restaurants that you must try while visiting. They will be worth keeping yourself full your entire trip!

# PACKING AND PLANNING TIPS

## A Week before Leaving

- Arrange for someone to take care of pets and water plants.

- Email and Print important Documents.

- Get Visa and vaccines if needed.

- Check for travel warnings.

- Stop mail and newspaper.

- Notify Credit Card companies where you are going.

- Passports and photo identification is up to date.

- Pay bills.

- Copy important items and download travel Apps.

- Start collecting small bills for tips.

- Have post office hold mail while you are away.

- Check weather for the week.

- Car inspected, oil is changed, and tires have the correct pressure.

- Check airline luggage restrictions.

- Download Apps needed for your trip.

# Right Before Leaving

- Contact bank and credit cards to tell them your location.

- Clean out refrigerator.

- Empty garbage cans.

- Lock windows.

- Make sure you have the proper identification with you.

- Bring cash for tips.

- Remember travel documents.

- Lock door behind you.

- Remember wallet.

- Unplug items in house and pack chargers.

- Change your thermostat settings.

- Charge electronics, and prepare camera memory cards.

# READ OTHER
# GREATER THAN A TOURIST
# BOOKS

*Greater Than a Tourist- Geneva Switzerland: 50 Travel Tips from a Local* by Amalia Kartika

*Greater Than a Tourist- St. Croix US Birgin Islands USA: 50 Travel Tips from a Local* by Tracy Birdsall

*Greater Than a Tourist- San Juan Puerto Rico: 50 Travel Tips from a Local* by Melissa Tait

*Greater Than a Tourist – Lake George Area New York USA: 50 Travel Tips from a Local* by Janine Hirschklau

*Greater Than a Tourist – Monterey California United States: 50 Travel Tips from a Local* by Katie Begley

*Greater Than a Tourist – Chanai Crete Greece: 50 Travel Tips from a Local* by Dimitra Papagrigoraki

*Greater Than a Tourist – The Garden Route Western Cape Province South Africa: 50 Travel Tips from a Local* by Li-Anne McGregor van Aardt

*Greater Than a Tourist – Sevilla Andalusia Spain: 50 Travel Tips from a Local* by Gabi Gazon

Children's Book: *Charlie the Cavalier Travels the World* by Lisa Rusczyk

57

# > TOURIST

Follow us on Instagram for beautiful travel images:
http://Instagram.com/GreaterThanATourist

Follow *Greater Than a Tourist* on Amazon.
>Tourist Podcast
>T Website
>T Youtube
>T Facebook
>T TikTok
>T Goodreads
>T Amazon
>T Mailing List
>T Pinterest
>T Instagram
>T Twitter
>T SoundCloud
>T LinkedIn
>T Map

# > TOURIST

At *Greater Than a Tourist*, we love to share travel tips with you. How did we do? What guidance do you have for how we can give you better advice for your next trip? Please send your feedback to GreaterThanaTourist@gmail.com as we continue to improve the series. We appreciate your constructive feedback. Thank you.

# METRIC CONVERSIONS

## TEMPERATURE

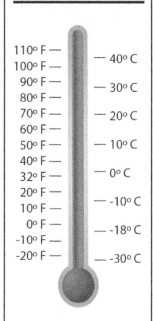

110° F —
100° F —      — 40° C
90° F —
80° F —       — 30° C
70° F —       — 20° C
60° F —
50° F —       — 10° C
40° F —
32° F —       — 0° C
20° F —
10° F —       — -10° C
0° F —
-10° F —      — -18° C
-20° F —      — -30° C

*To convert F to C:*

Subtract 32, and then multiply by 5/9 or .5555.

*To Convert C to F:*

Multiply by 1.8
and then add 32.

*32F = 0C*

## LIQUID VOLUME

**To Convert:...................Multiply by**
U.S. Gallons to Liters............... 3.8
U.S. Liters to Gallons ................26
Imperial Gallons to U.S. Gallons 1.2
Imperial Gallons to Liters....... 4.55
Liters to Imperial Gallons ........22
**1 Liter = .26 U.S. Gallon**
**1 U.S. Gallon = 3.8 Liters**

## DISTANCE

**To convert ............Multiply by**
Inches to Centimeters ....2.54
Centimeters to Inches ........39
Feet to Meters....................... .3
Meters to Feet ...................3.28
Yards to Meters ..................91
Meters to Yards ................1.09
Miles to Kilometers ..........1.61
Kilometers to Miles............ .62
**1 Mile = 1.6 km**
**1 km = .62 Miles**

## WEIGHT

1 Ounce = .28 Grams
1 Pound = .4555 Kilograms
1 Gram = .04 Ounce
1 Kilogram = 2.2 Pounds

# TRAVEL QUESTIONS

- Do you bring presents home to family or friends after a vacation?

- Do you get motion sick?

- Do you have a favorite billboard?

- Do you know what to do if there is a flat tire?

- Do you like a sun roof open?

- Do you like to eat in the car?

- Do you like to wear sun glasses in the car?

- Do you like toppings on your ice cream?

- Do you use public bathrooms?

- Did you bring your cell phone and does it have power?

- Do you have a form of identification with you?

- Have you ever been pulled over by a cop?

- Have you ever given money to a stranger on a road trip?

- Have you ever taken a road trip with animals?

- Have you ever went on a vacation alone?

- Have you ever run out of gas?

- If you could move to any place in the world, where would it be?

- If you could travel anywhere in the world, where would you travel?

- If you could travel in any vehicle, which one would it be?

- If you had three things to wish for from a magic genie, what would they be?

- If you have a driver's license, how many times did it take you to pass the test?

- What are you the most afraid of on vacation?

- What do you want to get away from the most when you are on vacation?

- What foods smells bad to you?

- What item do you bring on ever trip with you away from home?

- What makes you sleepy?

- What song would you love to hear on the radio when you're cruising on the highway?

- What travel job would you want the least?

- What will you miss most while you are away from home?

- What is something you always wanted to try?

- What is the best road side attraction that you ever saw?

- What is the farthest distance you ever biked?

- What is the farthest distance you ever walked?

- What is the weirdest thing you needed to buy while on vacation?

- What is your favorite candy?

- What is your favorite color car?

- What is your favorite family vacation?

- What is your favorite food?

- What is your favorite gas station drink or food?

- What is your favorite license plate design?

- What is your favorite restaurant?

- What is your favorite smell?

- What is your favorite song?

- What is your favorite sound that nature makes?

- What is your favorite thing to bring home from a vacation?

- What is your favorite vacation with friends?

- What is your favorite way to relax?

- Where is the farthest place you ever traveled in a car?

- Where is the farthest place you ever went North, South, East and West?

- Where is your favorite place in the world?

- Who is your favorite singer?

- Who taught you how to drive?

- Who will you miss the most while you are away?

- Who if the first person you will contact when you get to your destination?

- Who brought you on your first vacation?

- Who likes to travel the most in your life?

- Would you rather be hot or cold?

- Would you rather drive above, below, or at the speed limited?

- Would you rather drive on a highway or a back road?

- Would you rather go on a train or a boat?

- Would you rather go to the beach or the woods?

>TOURIST

# TRAVEL BUCKET LIST

1.

2.

3.

4.

5.

6.

7.

8.

9.

10.

# NOTES

Made in the USA
Monee, IL
16 November 2020

47994197R00049